Amazing Grace

© 2013 by Barbour Publishing, Inc.

Written and compiled by Jennifer Hahn.

Print ISBN 978-1-62416-146-9

eBook Editions:
Adobe Digital Edition (.epub) 978-1-62416-457-6
Kindle and MobiPocket Edition (.prc) 978-1-62416-456-9

Published by Barbour Publishing, Inc., P.O. Box 719, Uhrichsville, Ohio 44683, www.barbourbooks.com

Our mission is to publish and distribute inspirational products offering exceptional value and biblical encouragement to the masses.

Member of the
Evangelical Christian
Publishers Association

Printed in the United States of America.

Amazing Grace

Inspiration from the Beloved Hymn

BARBOUR
PUBLISHING

Contents

Amazing Grace

Amazing grace! How sweet the sound
That saved a wretch like me!
I once was lost, but now am found;
Was blind, but now I see.

'Twas grace that taught my heart to fear,
And grace my fears relieved;
How precious did that grace appear
The hour I first believed!

Through many dangers, toils and snares,
I have already come;
'Tis grace hath brought me safe thus far,
And grace will lead me home.

The Lord has promised good to me,
His Word my hope secures;
He will my shield and portion be,
As long as life endures.

Yea, when this flesh and heart shall fail,
And mortal life shall cease,
I shall possess, within the veil,
A life of joy and peace.

The earth shall soon dissolve like snow,
The sun forbear to shine;
But God, who called me here below,
Will be forever mine.

When we've been there ten thousand years,
Bright shining as the sun,
We've no less days to sing God's praise
Than when we'd first begun.

JOHN NEWTON, 1779

Amazing Grace!
How Sweet the Sound

*The grace of our Lord was poured out
on me abundantly, along with the faith
and love that are in Christ Jesus.*

1 TIMOTHY 1:14 NIV

The amazing grace of the Lord is beyond our understanding. Think of it: Adam and Eve, made by a loving Creator, enjoyed pure fellowship with Him in the Garden of Eden. But through an act of their will, sin entered in. What was a relationship of trust and love was ruined by the sinful nature of the very beings God created. Man and woman's disobedience created a barrier between them and God—but the story didn't end there.

The Creator, from His heart of love, provided a way to restore the relationship that had been lost. How? Through His grace—unmerited favor! God sent His Son to die so that believers could live forever with Him. He has given us what we don't deserve so that we can remain with Him in all ways—and for all our days! What a loving Savior!

This grace is nothing less than amazing. No logic can explain it. Nothing we could ever say or do could make us worthy. But the God of the universe—the One we sinned against—has put in place a plan that removes the curse of death. His sacrifice gives us freedom. His pain brings us healing. His death grants us life. That is unfathomable, amazing grace!

Grace, mercy and peace will be with us,
from God the Father and from Jesus Christ,
the Son of the Father, in truth and love.

2 JOHN 1:3 NASB

✦

Out of his fullness we have all received
grace in place of grace already given.

JOHN 1:16 NIV

✦

The Word became flesh and made his
dwelling among us. We have seen his glory,
the glory of the one and only Son, who came
from the Father, full of grace and truth.

JOHN 1:14 NIV

GRACE:
God's
Riches
At
Christ's
Expense.
<small>UNKNOWN</small>

❦

Once I knew what it was to rest upon
the rock of God's promises, and it was
indeed a precious resting place, but now I
rest in His grace. He is teaching me that the
bosom of His love is a far sweeter resting-place
than even the rock of His promises.

<small>HANNAH WHITALL SMITH</small>

For the law was given through Moses;
grace and truth came through Jesus Christ.

For the grace of God has been revealed,
bringing salvation to all people.

But the gift is not like the
trespass. For if the many
died by the trespass of the
one man, how much more
did God's grace and the gift
that came by the grace of
the one man, Jesus Christ,
overflow to the many!

Gratitude for Grace

Heavenly Father, thank You for Your grace.
I realize I have done nothing to earn it. In
Your goodness, You have reached out to me
and saved me from my sin. Forgive me for
the times I take Your gift for granted and act
as if I've done something to deserve it. Help
me to accept Your grace with a sincere heart,
yet without guilt, as You have promised me
forgiveness when I repent. Your grace is
indeed amazing! Amen.

And God will generously provide all you need.
Then you will always have everything you need
and plenty left over to share with others.

2 CORINTHIANS 9:8 NLT

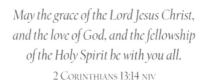

May the grace of the Lord Jesus Christ,
and the love of God, and the fellowship
of the Holy Spirit be with you all.

2 CORINTHIANS 13:14 NIV

A man can no more take in a supply of
grace for the future than he can eat enough
today to last him for the next 6 months,
nor can he inhale sufficient air into his lungs
with one breath to sustain life for a week to come.
We are permitted to draw upon God's store of
grace from day to day as we need it.

D. L. Moody

The law detects,
grace alone conquers sin.

Saint Augustine of Hippo

Abounding sin is the terror
of the world, but abounding
grace is the hope of mankind.

A. W. Tozer

For sin shall not have dominion over you,
for you are not under the law but under grace.

ROMANS 6:14 NKJV

❧

God's law was given so that all people could see how
sinful they were. But as people sinned more and more,
God's wonderful grace became more abundant. So
just as sin ruled over all people and brought them
to death, now God's wonderful grace rules instead,
giving us right standing with God and resulting in
eternal life through Jesus Christ our Lord.

ROMANS 5:20–21 NET

Grace to Me,
Grace to Others

Lord, I ask that You give me the
strength to extend grace to others as
You have so freely extended it to me.
I confess that I often react in
accordance with how others have
treated me. I respond to their words
or actions in the way that I feel is fair.
But that is not a demonstration of
the grace You exemplify. May my
life mirror the grace that You
have shown to me. Amen.

Grace is free sovereign
favor to the ill-deserving.

BENJAMIN B. WARFIELD

As heat is opposed to cold,
and light to darkness,
so grace is opposed to sin.

THOMAS BENTON BROOKS

We believe that the work of
regeneration, conversion,
sanctification and faith, is not
an act of man's free will and power,
but of the mighty, efficacious
and irresistible grace of God.

CHARLES SPURGEON

*That Saved a
Wretch Like Me!*

What a wretched man I am!
Who will rescue me from this body
that is subject to death?

ROMANS 7:24 NIV

Wretch. The word itself sounds so unlovely—
certainly not a term that anyone would choose
to describe himself. Focusing so much time and
attention on our outward appearance, in an attempt
to have beautiful skin, hair, and body, we balk at the
thought that someone could consider us despicable.
Yet because of the deceitfulness of our hearts, the
term *wretched* describes us quite accurately.

Our outer personae is a glossy cover to a heart that may harbor pride, selfishness, envy, hatred, unforgiveness—and more. Yet our maker can see beyond our façade to the black marks of sin within.

But because of His love, Christ provided a way to save us from ourselves. Although wretched in heart, humanity to Him was worthy of His sacrifice. Our sin stains are washed away by the blood of Jesus, shed to cleanse the very hearts that chose to wander from Him. How humbling that is! In His compassion, He took on the unlovely heart and has found it lovely.

For God did not send the Son into the world
to judge the world, but that the world
might be saved through Him.

JOHN 3:17 NASB

"My grace is sufficient for you,
for My strength is made perfect in weakness."
Therefore most gladly I will rather boast in my infirmities,
that the power of Christ may rest upon me.

2 CORINTHIANS 12:9 NKJV

Only those who have learned well to be
earnestly dissatisfied with themselves,
and to be confounded with shame at their
wretchedness truly understand
the Christian gospel.

JOHN CALVIN

Many are convinced, who are not truly enlightened;
are afraid of the consequences of sin,
though they never saw its evil; have a seeming
desire of salvation, which is not founded
upon a truly spiritual discovery of their own
wretchedness, and the excellency of Jesus.

JOHN NEWTON

"You say, 'I am rich; I have acquired wealth and
do not need a thing.' But you do not realize that
you are wretched, pitiful, poor, blind and naked."

REVELATION 3:17 NIV

I am worn out calling for help; my throat is parched.
My eyes fail, looking for my God.

PSALM 69:3 NIV

Wretchedness

Lord Jesus, I admit that, at times,
my heart is wretched. My sin brings grief
to You and creates a barrier between us.
Yet You have assured me that
You will forgive me when I repent.
The relationship between the wretched
creature and the loving Creator is
restored. You are perfect; I am imperfect.
You are love; I am unlovely. Thank You
for looking beyond my sin and seeing
the person—body, soul, and spirit—You
created me to be. In Your name, amen.

*"We believe it is through the grace of
our Lord Jesus that we are saved."*

✦

*For by grace you have been saved through faith;
and that not of yourselves, it is the gift of God;
not as a result of works, so that no one may boast.
For we are His workmanship, created in Christ Jesus
for good works, which God prepared
beforehand so that we would walk in them.*

Ephesians 2:8–10 NASB

Grace is the good pleasure of God
that inclines him to bestow benefits
upon the undeserving. . . .
Its use to us sinful men is to save us
and make us sit together in heavenly
places to demonstrate to the ages
the exceeding riches of God's
kindness to us in Christ Jesus.

A. W. TOZER

A man must completely despair of himself in order
to become fit to obtain the grace of Christ.

MARTIN LUTHER

"And it shall be that everyone who calls on the name of the Lord will be saved."

ACTS 2:21 NASB

❧

He saved us, not on the basis of deeds which we have done in righteousness, but according to His mercy, by the washing of regeneration and renewing by the Holy Spirit.

TITUS 3:5 NASB

Beautiful to God

Heavenly Father, thank You for Your
salvation. There is nothing that I could
have ever done or will ever be able to do to
earn my way to You. Yet I need not come to
despair over my humanness because You
have provided me a way out through Christ.
Thank You for loving me so much that
You sent Jesus to die in my place.
And thank You that, in Your eyes,
my heart is beautiful and precious. Amen.

Grace is the free, undeserved goodness
and favor of God to mankind.

MATTHEW HENRY

All outward means of grace, if separate
from the spirit of God, cannot profit,
or conduce, in any degree,
either to the knowledge or love of God.
All outward things, unless he work
in them and by them, are in vain.

JOHN WESLEY

Free grace can go into the gutter,
and bring up a jewel!

CHARLES SPURGEON

*I Once Was Lost,
but Now Am Found*

"For the Son of Man came to seek and to save the lost."
LUKE 19:10 NIV

⟨⟩

Getting lost is a lonely, frightening feeling. A child who wanders from his mother and cannot find his way back to her not only produces panic in himself, but in his mother as well. The two individuals who have long been a part of each other feel sorrow until they are reunited.

Oh, the anguish the Father must have felt when His Son left Him to go to earth! Father and Son, who had been unified in heaven, were now separated. But God willed that Jesus come down to do an incredibly valuable act for humankind. Then the day finally came that the one Son would be sacrificed for all. The impact of taking on the sin of the world caused Jesus' Father to have to turn His back on His only Son. What grief!

But then what joy! Jesus conquered the sorrow. He was victorious over death and returned to heaven, reunited once again with the Father. And because of His selfless act we, who were once separated from God because of our sin, can now have a relationship with Him. There is no more fear or anguish. Praise the Lord that we who have sought God are no longer lost, but found!

"This son of mine was dead and has now returned to life.
He was lost, but now he is found."

LUKE 15:24 NLT

Behold, I stand at the door, and knock:
if any man hear my voice, and open the door,
I will come in to him, and will sup
with him, and he with me.

REVELATION 3:20 KJV

To be lost is to live in an unregenerate condition,
loveless and unloved; and to be saved is to love;
he that dwelleth in love dwelleth already in God.
For God is Love.

HENRY DRUMMOND

❦

Jesus Christ became Incarnate for one purpose,
to make a way back to God that man might
stand before Him as He was created to do,
the friend and lover of God Himself.

OSWALD CHAMBERS

❦

Christ took our sins and the sins of the whole
world as well as the Father's wrath on his
shoulders, and he has drowned them both in
himself so that we are thereby reconciled to God
and become completely righteous.

MARTIN LUTHER

"What man among you, if he has a hundred sheep
and has lost one of them, does not leave the
ninety-nine in the open pasture and go after
the one which is lost until he finds it?
When he has found it. . .he calls together
his friends and his neighbors, saying to them,
'Rejoice with me, for I have found my sheep
which was lost!' I tell you that in the same way,
there will be more joy in heaven over one sinner
who repents than over ninety-nine righteous
persons who need no repentance."

LUKE 15:4–7 NASB

The Gift of Jesus

Dear Father, thank You for willingly
allowing Your Son to come to earth.
That must have caused You such
great anguish. To send Him from the
perfection of heaven, to have Him leave
Your side would have been sorrow
enough. But You then gave Him up
and let Him take on sin that
You couldn't even look upon.
I'm amazed that You found me
worthy of saving. You've given me a
gift I never can repay. Thank You for
retrieving me—mind, body, and soul.
I want to stay close to You so
that we are never again separated.
May I keep my heart pure and in
communion with Yours. Amen.

"What woman, if she has ten silver coins and loses one coin, does not light a lamp and sweep the house and search carefully until she finds it? When she has found it, she calls together her friends and neighbors, saying, 'Rejoice with me, for I have found the coin which I had lost!' In the same way, I tell you, there is joy in the presence of the angels of God over one sinner who repents."

LUKE 15:8–10 NASB

Christ is the breathing forth of the
heart, life and spirit of God into all the
dead race of Adam. He is the seeker,
the finder, the restorer of all that,
from Cain to the end of time, was lost
and dead to the life of God. He is the
love that. . .wants and seeks to forgive
where most is to be forgiven.

WILLIAM LAW

Grace is love that cares and
stoops and rescues.

JOHN R. W. STOTT

And I am convinced that nothing can ever separate us from God's love. Neither death nor life, neither angels nor demons, neither our fears for today nor our worries about tomorrow— not even the powers of hell can separate us from God's love. No power in the sky above or in the earth below—indeed, nothing in all creation will ever be able to separate us from the love of God that is revealed in Christ Jesus our Lord.

ROMANS 8:38–39 NLT

Now I'm Found

Jesus, oh the joy of being sought, then found!
It is indeed a time of jubilation, a rejoicing
that what was once separated is now restored
and will never be alienated from You again.
Thank You for pursuing me and finding me.
I give to You my whole heart—my whole
being—to use for Your glory. I want to be
worthy of the joy You found in saving me
from my sins. In Your name, amen.

Forgiveness is the remission of sins.
For it is by this that what has been lost,
and was found, is saved from being lost again.

Saint Augustine of Hippo

Either sin is with you, lying on your shoulders,
or it is lying on Christ, the Lamb of God.
Now if it is lying on your back, you are lost;
but if it is resting on Christ, you are free,
and you will be saved.
Now choose what you want.

Martin Luther

Was Blind, but Now I See

*"I have come as a light to shine in this dark world,
so that all who put their trust in me
will no longer remain in the dark."*

JOHN 12:46 NLT

Have you ever tried to walk through your house
in complete darkness? Without even a glimmer
of light, all you can see is blackness, regardless of
how much you squint. You know vaguely where
pieces of furniture and walls are, but you cannot
distinguish them. You grope around to feel any
hidden dangers that may trip you up. The anxiety
that you could run into something, stub a toe,
or fall flat on your face is very real.

That's a little like our spiritual life, before salvation. Prior to accepting Christ, we try to make it through the darkness of sin independently, steering around unseen dangers. But tragedy is certain without a Savior. Without sight—and light—we cannot safely reach the destination.

But the moment we believe, God brings full sight to our eyes that had previously failed. The path now becomes clear. Fear subsides. Our days of wandering aimlessly are over. The destination is evident. One look at the Savior's face brings comfort and strength. And spiritual eyes are finally opened to see all the Father has in store for believers.

Make your ear attentive to wisdom,
incline your heart to understanding;
for if you cry for discernment, lift your voice for
understanding; if you seek her as silver and search for her
as for hidden treasures; then you will discern the fear of
the LORD and discover the knowledge of God.

PROVERBS 2:2–5 NASB

Give me understanding,
so that I may keep your law and
obey it with all my heart.

PSALM 119:34 NIV

Knowledge is but folly unless
it is guided by grace.

GEORGE HERBERT

We can't have full knowledge all
at once. We must start by believing;
then afterwards we may be led on to
master the evidence for ourselves.

THOMAS AQUINAS

And when he comes, he will open the eyes of the blind and unplug the ears of the deaf. The lame will leap like a deer, and those who cannot speak will sing for joy! Springs will gush forth in the wilderness, and streams will water the wasteland. The parched ground will become a pool, and springs of water will satisfy the thirsty land.

ISAIAH 35:5–7 NLT

Blind No More

Lord Jesus, I do not think I realized how in
the dark I was. I know where I am now in my
relationship with You, and I have come so far
from where I had been. Without You, my life
would have no purpose. I would not know
real love. Because of Your grace, Your gift of
salvation has brought meaning to my life,
and I know the one who is Light.
Thank You for taking away my blindness!
In Your name, amen.

If any of you lacks wisdom, you should ask God,
who gives generously to all without finding fault,
and it will be given to you.

JAMES 1:5 NIV

"No eye has seen, no ear has heard, and no mind has
imagined what God has prepared for those who love him."
But it was to us that God revealed these things by his Spirit.
For his Spirit searches out everything
and shows us God's deep secrets.

1 CORINTHIANS 2:9–10 NLT

Acquaint yourself with your own ignorance.

ISAAC WATTS

If I am walking along the street with
a very disfiguring hole in the back of my dress,
of which I am in ignorance, it is certainly a very
great comfort to me to have a kind friend who will
tell me of it. And similarly it is indeed a comfort to
know that there is always abiding with me a divine,
all-seeing Comforter, who will reprove me for all
my faults, and will not let me go on in
a fatal unconsciousness of them.

HANNAH WHITALL SMITH

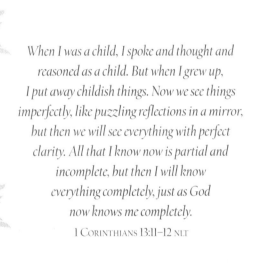

When I was a child, I spoke and thought and reasoned as a child. But when I grew up, I put away childish things. Now we see things imperfectly, like puzzling reflections in a mirror, but then we will see everything with perfect clarity. All that I know now is partial and incomplete, but then I will know everything completely, just as God now knows me completely.

1 Corinthians 13:11–12 NLT

Now I See!

Dear Father, what a joy! I can now see!
Your light has come into my life and has overcome
the darkness of my heart. Thank You for saving
me. Because of Your Son's sacrifice, I am no longer
sentenced to eternal death and darkness—
You have given me everlasting life and light!
The change is like going from blindness to sight.
My spirit is renewed and barriers removed.
I am ready to explore my enlightened path, the one
You have laid before me. In Jesus' name, amen.

God does not so much want us to do things
as to let people see what He can do.

A. B. Simpson

What I am anxious to see in Christian
believers is a beautiful paradox.
I want to see in them the joy of finding God
while at the same time they are blessedly
pursuing Him. I want to see in them the great
joy of having God yet always wanting Him.

A. W. Tozer

The Hour I First Believed!

"For God so loved the world,
that He gave His only begotten Son,
that whoever believes in Him shall not perish,
but have eternal life.

JOHN 3:16 NASB

Time dictates so much in life. There are clocks,
electronic devices, and watches that constantly
remind us of the hour. In our harried schedules,
it's easy to be carried away by the clock. Chores,
errands, and responsibilities are dictated by the
ticking of old timepieces or pulsing of the new. And
at day's end we attempt to recharge, with the hope
of having enough stamina to make it through the
routine the following day.

But in the Christian life, there is a definite shift in time—a moment when everything suddenly changes. The mundane ticking has faded away and things are different. It's the hour we first believe! The focus shifts from ourselves to God. Following the ways of the world has ended; pursuing a life with Jesus has begun. All of the old is gone; new life in Jesus is here!

How simple it is over time, however, to return to that old, familiar ticking—our way of life before Jesus interceded. The feeling of newness can fade. The routine can become stagnant.

Our Lord is patient and waits for us to reignite that fire. Today, decide to return to Him with the same passion you had the hour you first believed.

Seek the LORD while he may be found;
call on him while he is near.

❧

But as many as received Him, to them
He gave the right to become children of God,
even to those who believe in His name.

JOHN 1:12 NASB

❧

"Believe in the Lord Jesus,
and you will be saved—you and your household."

ACTS 16:31 NIV

I believe in Christianity as I believe that
the sun has risen: not only because I see it,
but because by it I see everything else.

C. S. LEWIS

He who created us without our help
will not save us without our consent.

SAINT AUGUSTINE OF HIPPO

So often we have a kind of vague, wistful longing
that the promises of Jesus should be true. The only
way really to enter into them is to believe them with
the clutching intensity of a drowning man.

WILLIAM BARCLAY

He came as a witness, to testify about the Light,
so that all might believe through him.

JOHN 1:7 NASB

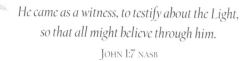

"Truly, truly, I say to you, he who hears My word,
and believes Him who sent Me, has eternal life,
and does not come into judgment,
but has passed out of death into life."

JOHN 5:24 NASB

The Hour of Belief

Heavenly Father, thank You for the hour I first believed. I am awed You loved me so much that You prepared a way for me to come to You and enjoy a relationship with You. Please help me not to become complacent in my spiritual walk. May the joy of fellowship mark each moment of my days as I cling to You and Your Word. May I wake tomorrow with even more excitement at the thought of communing with You. In Jesus' name, amen.

If you confess with your mouth Jesus as Lord,
and believe in your heart that God raised Him
from the dead, you will be saved.

ROMANS 10:9 NASB

"I do believe; help my unbelief."

MARK 9:24 NASB

"Yes, Lord," she replied, "I believe that you are the Messiah,
the Son of God, who is to come into the world."

JOHN 11:27 NIV

A man's real belief is that
which he lives by.
What a man believes is
the thing he does,
not the thing he thinks.

GEORGE MACDONALD

Sight is not faith, and hearing is not faith,
neither is feeling faith; but believing
when we neither see, hear, nor feel is
faith; and everywhere the Bible
tells us our salvation is to be by faith.
Therefore we must believe before we feel,
and often against our feelings, if we
would honor God by our faith.

HANNAH WHITALL SMITH

Jesus said to her,
"I am the resurrection and the life.
The one who believes in me will live,
even though they die."

JOHN 11:25 NIV

Everyone who believes in him
will have eternal life.

JOHN 3:15 NLT

But these are written that you may believe
that Jesus is the Messiah, the Son of God,
and that by believing you
may have life in his name.

JOHN 20:31 NIV

Renewed Passion

Lord Jesus, I want to have priority time with You each day, not just spend with You what time is left after all the demands upon me have been met. Give me the wisdom to view my schedule and responsibilities with You always in mind, knowing that I am to seek You first in all things. When I do, everything else will fall in place and I will find myself renewed with the passion I had "the hour I first believed." In Your name, amen.

You never know how much you really believe
anything until its truth or falsehood
becomes a matter of life and death to you.

C. S. Lewis

Jesus is not one of many ways to approach God,
nor is He the best of several ways;
He is the only way.

A. W. Tozer

There is either of two things we must do.
One is to send back the message to heaven
that we don't want the blood of Christ
to cleanse us of our sin, or else accept it.

D. L. Moody

Through Many Dangers. . .
I Have Already Come

We can rejoice, too, when we run into problems and trials,
for we know that they help us develop endurance.
And endurance develops strength of character,
and character strengthens our confident hope of salvation.

ROMANS 5:3–4 NLT

Adversity will affect each person's life at some
point and can come in different forms—financial
troubles, health issues, and the loss of loved ones.
Unexpected trials can quickly sweep in, touching a
life with grief or anguish.

Temptation can also come at any moment.
If given in to, confusion and consequences can
follow in its wake. And there are other countless,
unforeseen dangers that have the potential of
changing the course of one's life.

But in all of these times of challenge, we can be assured that nothing will reach God's child without His knowledge. He does not cause the difficulty but is prepared to walk with His child through it and provide strength when all human power is gone.

What looks like a hopeless situation to the world can be a season that brings the believer even closer to her Lord. She, at the end of that challenging season, can savor a sweet time of victory and glory to the One who walked, or even carried, her through.

Because we live in a world touched by sin, sorrow will affect both unbeliever and believer alike. But what a hope we who are in Christ have! We can draw close to the Savior and rest in the comfort and peace that only He can give amid the storm.

He who began a good work in you will carry it on
to completion until the day of Christ Jesus.

PHILIPPIANS 1:6 NIV

❦

I can do all things through Him
who strengthens me.

PHILIPPIANS 4:13 NASB

❦

I consider that our present sufferings
are not worth comparing with
the glory that will be revealed in us.

ROMANS 8:18 NIV

Bad Times. . .Good Times?

Heavenly Father, it is difficult to look at adversity
as something potentially good for me. I'd prefer to
avoid it all costs. However, in times of hardship,
I know I can run to You, drawing closer in my time
of need. Please strengthen me so that when the
tough times come, I don't try to escape them,
but stand strong, knowing You are with me, ready
to lift me up and carry me, if need be. Amen.

The LORD hears his people when they call to him for help.
He rescues them from all their troubles.
The LORD is close to the brokenhearted;
he rescues those whose spirits are crushed.
The righteous person faces many troubles,
but the LORD comes to the rescue each time.
For the LORD protects the bones of the righteous;
not one of them is broken!

PSALM 34:17–20 NLT

And we know that God causes everything
to work together for the good of those who love God
and are called according to his purpose for them.

ROMANS 8:28 NLT

In times of affliction we commonly meet with
the sweetest experiences of the love of God.

JOHN BUNYAN

God delights to increase the faith of His children.
. . .We ought, instead of wanting no trials before
victory, no exercise for patience, to be willing
to take them from God's hands as a means. . . .
Trials, obstacles, difficulties and sometimes
defeats, are the very food of faith.

GEORGE MÜELLER

No temptation has overtaken you but such
as is common to man; and God is faithful,
who will not allow you to be tempted beyond
what you are able, but with the temptation
will provide the way of escape also,
so that you will be able to endure it.

1 CORINTHIANS 10:13 NASB

Therefore we do not lose heart,
but though our outer man is decaying,
yet our inner man is being renewed day by day.

2 CORINTHIANS 4:16 NASB

Increasing My Faith

Lord Jesus, thank You for increasing my faith
in the midst of "dangers, toils, and snares."
At times the weight of trials threatens to
overcome me, but that is when I turn to You
and ask for help. Please open my eyes so that
I can see what You are teaching me. I want to
be a wise student, grasping whatever lesson
You have for me the first time around. Thank
You for being so patient and walking so close
to me in the darkest of valleys. Amen.

Therefore, since we are surrounded by such a great cloud of witnesses, let us throw off everything that hinders and the sin that so easily entangles. And let us run with perseverance the race marked out for us.

HEBREWS 12:1 NIV

❧

As you know, we count as blessed those who have persevered. You have heard of Job's perseverance and have seen what the Lord finally brought about. The Lord is full of compassion and mercy.

JAMES 5:11 NIV

Christian, remember the goodness
of God in the frost of adversity.

CHARLES SPURGEON

We are always in the forge,
or on the anvil;
by trials God is shaping us
for higher things.

HENRY WARD BEECHER

Trials come to prove and improve us.

SAINT AUGUSTINE OF HIPPO

"These things I have spoken to you,
that in Me you may have peace.
In the world you will have tribulation;
but be of good cheer,
I have overcome the world."

JOHN 16:33 NKJV

*

Give your burdens to the LORD,
and he will take care of you.
He will not permit the godly to slip and fall.

PSALM 55:22 NLT

The Hardships of Others

Lord Jesus, show me how I can help someone
else who is experiencing a difficult situation. In
fact, help me to be intentional in seeking out the
hurting, and may I not only pray for them, but offer
the assistance they may require. May such caring
for others undergoing hardship reflect Your light
so that they will ultimately see You as the source of
love and glorify Your hand in their lives. Amen.

The bottom of the soul may be in repose,
even while we are in many outward troubles;
just as the bottom of the sea is calm,
while the surface is strongly agitated.

JOHN WESLEY

Adversity is always unexpected and
unwelcomed. It is an intruder and a thief,
and yet in the hands of God, adversity
becomes the means through which
His supernatural power is demonstrated.

CHARLES STANLEY

'Tis Grace Hath Brought Me
Safe Thus Far

Let us then approach God's throne of grace
with confidence, so that we may receive mercy
and find grace to help us in our time of need.

HEBREWS 4:16 NIV

An adult will often prepare to cross a street with
a cursory glance left and right for oncoming traffic
before crossing. A child, however, needs help
in getting from one side to the other. Although
the child may think he can dodge traffic by
himself, most kids—because of their size, limited
experience, and not-yet-fully-developed peripheral
vision—just don't have the ability to see all the
dangers of oncoming traffic. With someone to hold
his hand and lead, the child will reach the other
side of the street safe and sound.

So it is with God. He can see the dangers around us, His children, and knows the best path for us to take. He offers His hand to lead us through potential unseen risks and guides us safely to our destination.

Our Savior will gently lead you through troubles, but there are also times that His gracious hand will pick you up. The path may seem too long and tiring. Human strength can fail, and it is at those moments that God will lovingly carry you through the difficulty.

*But to each one of us grace has been
given as Christ apportioned it.*

Ephesians 4:7 niv

*All are justified freely by his grace through
the redemption that came by Christ Jesus.*

Romans 3:24 niv

*I became a servant of this gospel
by the gift of God's grace given me
through the working of his power.*

Ephesians 3:7 niv

My Walking Partner

Lord Jesus, thank You for the gracious
way You care for me. Your faithfulness and
gentleness have brought me this far along
my life's path, and I am confident that You
will not leave me now. You partner with me,
walking beside me all the way, leading me in
the paths I should go and keeping me from
harm. I have full assurance that I can entrust
my life to You and to Your direction.
In Your name, amen.

In him we have redemption through his blood,
the forgiveness of sins, in accordance with the
riches of God's grace that he lavished on us.

Ephesians 1:7–8 NIV

❦

What shall we say, then?
Shall we go on sinning so that grace
may increase? By no means!
We are those who have died to sin;
how can we live in it any longer?

Romans 6:1–2 NIV

As mercy is God's goodness
confronting human misery and guilt,
so grace is his goodness directed
toward human debt and demerit.

A. W. TOZER

❧

Saving faith is an immediate relation
to Christ, accepting, receiving, resting
upon Him alone, for justification,
sanctification, and eternal life
by virtue of God's grace.

CHARLES SPURGEON

The gospel is bearing fruit and growing
throughout the whole world—just as it
has been doing among you since the day you
heard it and truly understood God's grace.

COLOSSIANS 1:6 NIV

He has saved us and called us to a holy life—not
because of anything we have done but because of
his own purpose and grace. This grace was given
us in Christ Jesus before the beginning of time.

2 TIMOTHY 1:9 NIV

My Repentant Heart

Dear Jesus, I repent of the times that
I have given in to temptation and sin,
knowing all the while that You would extend
grace when I asked for Your forgiveness. That is
an abuse of Your goodness. It is hard and shameful
to admit that I, at times, knowingly sin—yet You
already know my heart for nothing is hidden from
You. Please give me the strength to avoid sin and
temptation so that your purpose for me is not
waylaid by my less-than-wise choices. Amen.

For if, by the trespass of the one man,
death reigned through that one man,
how much more will those who receive God's
abundant provision of grace and of the gift
of righteousness reign in life through
the one man, Jesus Christ!

ROMANS 5:17 NIV

⁓

But by the grace of God I am what I am,
and his grace to me was not without effect.
No, I worked harder than all of them—yet not I,
but the grace of God that was with me.

1 CORINTHIANS 15:10 NIV

I am a most noteworthy sinner, but I have cried
out to the Lord for grace and mercy, and they have
covered me completely. I have found the sweetest
consolation since I made it my whole purpose
to enjoy His marvelous Presence.

CHRISTOPHER COLUMBUS

Grace is God himself, his loving energy at work
within his church and within our souls.

EVELYN UNDERHILL

*Therefore, since we have been justified
through faith, we have peace with
God through our Lord Jesus Christ,
through whom we have gained access by
faith into this grace in which we now stand.
And we boast in the hope of the glory of God.*

ROMANS 5:1–2 NIV

*But grow in the grace and
knowledge of our Lord and
Savior Jesus Christ.
To him be glory both now and forever!
Amen.*

2 PETER 3:18 NIV

Growing in Grace and Knowledge

Heavenly Father, Your Word instructs me to keep growing in the grace and knowledge of Christ. Help me to do so. Reveal Your Word to me so that I can know You inside out. As I abide in and enjoy Your familiar presence, increase my faith so that I can do all the work You have prepared for me. As I grow in You, may all of the glory be Yours both now and forever. In Jesus' name, amen.

Once more, Never think that you can live
to God by your own power or strength;
but always look to and rely on him for
assistance, yea, for all strength and grace.

DAVID BRAINERD

Grace can pardon our ungodliness and justify
us with Christ's righteousness; it can put the
Spirit of Jesus Christ within us; it can help us
when we are down; it can heal us when we
are wounded; it can multiply pardons, as we,
through frailty, multiply transgressions.

JOHN BUNYAN

And Grace Will
Lead Me Home

Being justified by his grace, we should be made heirs
according to the hope of eternal life.

TITUS 3:7 KJV

❦

You may travel for your job or for personal pleasure. Perhaps you have saved a lifetime for a special vacation to an exotic location. Or maybe it's a destination that has been slated to spend with family. Whether the goal of the trip is to secure a deal for the employer, enjoy magnificent scenery, or spend moments away from the hustle and bustle of life, there is one commonality that unites all travelers: the joy of returning home. No matter how much pleasure you may get in your time away, for most of us it's true that there's no place like home.

After this journey of life upon the earth, we, as God's children, will finally reach our destination—a home with Jesus Christ. He has been preparing for and awaiting our arrival. This heavenly home will be a place of perfection and joy, a place where Creator and created can relax together after the journey. What a blessing it will be to have the Savior look into our eyes and say, "Welcome home, child. I have been waiting for you."

*Nevertheless we, according to His promise,
look for new heavens and a new earth
in which righteousness dwells.*

<small>2 PETER 3:13 NKJV</small>

*"Look! I am creating new heavens and
a new earth, and no one will even think
about the old ones anymore."*

<small>ISAIAH 65:17 NLT</small>

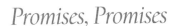

Promises, Promises

Thank You, Lord, for every one of Your
promises. So many have been kept and I'm
amazed that still more are to be fulfilled.
I look forward to the promise of heaven,
for You have declared You are preparing a
place there for me. I anticipate the day I am
ushered into Your presence and You welcome
me in, to spend eternity there, at home,
with You. In Jesus' name, amen.

And I saw the holy city, the new Jerusalem,
coming down from God out of heaven like
a bride beautifully dressed for her husband.
I heard a loud shout from the throne, saying,
"Look, God's home is now among his people!
He will live with them, and they will be his people.
God himself will be with them."

REVELATION 21:2–3 NLT

For we know that if the earthly
tent we live in is destroyed,
we have a building from God,
an eternal house in heaven,
not built by human hands.

2 CORINTHIANS 5:1 NIV

I do not at all understand
the mystery of grace—only that it
meets us where we are but does not
leave us where it found us.

ANNE LAMOTT

Grace comes into the soul,
as the morning sun into the world;
first a dawning, then a light;
and at last the sun in his full
and excellent brightness.

THOMAS ADAMS

For by the grace given me
I say to every one of you:
Do not think of yourself
more highly than you ought,
but rather think of yourself
with sober judgment,
in accordance with the faith God
has distributed to each of you.

ROMANS 12:3 NIV

We pleaded with you,
encouraged you, and urged you
to live your lives in a way that
God would consider worthy.
For he called you to share in
his Kingdom and glory.

1 THESSALONIANS 2:12 NLT

Fulfilling My Purpose

Father God, while I await being called to
heaven, I ask for wisdom and insight so that
I will be about Your business here on earth.
Each day I feel a little bit more like an alien
in this world and that my true home is with
You, but I know You have a purpose for me
while I am here. May I stay so close to You
that I can hear You whisper, "My child,
this way," in any moment of any day.
In Jesus' name, amen.

Then shall the King say unto them on his right hand,
Come, ye blessed of my Father, inherit the kingdom
prepared for you from the foundation of the world.

MATTHEW 25:34 KJV

❧

Then God will give you a grand entrance into the eternal
Kingdom of our Lord and Savior Jesus Christ.

2 PETER 1:11 NLT

❧

For Christ also died for sins once for all, the just for the
unjust, so that He might bring us to God, having been
put to death in the flesh, but made alive in the spirit.

1 PETER 3:18 NASB

The greater perfection a soul aspires after,
the more dependent it is upon divine grace.

BROTHER LAWRENCE

Lord, it belongs not to my care,
whether I die or live; to love and serve
Thee is my share, and this Thy grace must give.

RICHARD BAXTER

You will show me the path of life;
in Your presence is fullness of joy;
at Your right hand are pleasures forevermore.

PSALM 16:11 NKJV

When Christ, who is our life, is revealed,
then you also will be revealed with Him in glory.

COLOSSIANS 3:4 NASB

You will guide me with Your counsel,
and afterward receive me to glory.

PSALM 73:24 NKJV

The Lord Has Promised
Good to Me

Give thanks to the LORD, for he is good.

PSALM 136:1 NIV

❧

God has promised good. He does not guarantee that only good things will happen, simply that everything that comes from Him will be worked out for good in the life of the believer. We will be parted from loved ones by death. A job that we've had for ten years may be lost. Illness or injury will touch our lives. From a human perspective, none of these things seem "good" and may bring overwhelming grief.

But God's ways are so different from ours. What we view as a tragedy, Christ can use as a catalyst to bring about His great work. If a loved one chooses salvation as a result of our trial, can we then see the goodness? If, after we've suffered a loss, a wayward son or daughter returns to the Savior, does that lessen the grief in a small way?

Entrusting our life to the Lord is a daily act of discipline. He will shower blessings of goodness on His believers. And He will take hardships and use them for His good—and ours, although we may not see it until years down the road, if at all. He has promised goodness. And we, as His followers, must choose to fully trust Him, for He always keeps His promises.

For all of God's promises have been fulfilled in Christ with a resounding "Yes!" And through Christ, our "Amen" (which means "Yes") ascends to God for his glory.

2 CORINTHIANS 1:20 NLT

"Know therefore that the LORD your God, He is God, the faithful God, who keeps His covenant and His lovingkindness to a thousandth generation with those who love Him and keep His commandments."

DEUTERONOMY 7:9 NASB

Whatsoever is good;
the same is also approved of God.

RICHARD HOOKER

It is not the will of God to give us more
troubles than will bring us to live by faith
on him; he loves us too well to give us a
moment of uneasiness but for our good.

WILLIAM ROMAINE

God judged it better to bring good
out of evil than to suffer no evil to exist.

SAINT AUGUSTINE OF HIPPO

He was fully convinced that God
is able to do whatever he promises.

ROMANS 4:21 NLT

"Heaven and earth will pass away,
but My words will by no means pass away."

MATTHEW 24:35 NKJV

O taste and see that the LORD is good:
blessed is the man that trusteth in him.

PSALM 34:8 KJV

God's Promises

Jesus, Your Word reveals that You have good things in store for me. In Your goodness, You saved me by Your grace. You love me with unconditional, everlasting love. You are slow to get angry with me. You meet my physical, emotional, mental, and spiritual needs. Your ways are so much higher than mine. Because of all this I continue to trust that You will keep me in Your care today and forevermore. In Your name, amen.

He remains faithful,
for He cannot deny Himself.

2 TIMOTHY 2:13 NASB

❦

But you, O LORD, are a God
of compassion and mercy,
slow to get angry and filled
with unfailing love
and faithfulness.

PSALM 86:15 NLT

God is always trying
to give good things to us,
but our hands are too
full to receive them.

SAINT AUGUSTINE OF HIPPO

No good work is done
anywhere without aid
from the Father of Lights.

C. S. LEWIS

Christian humility does
not consist in denying
what there is of good in us;
but in an abiding sense of ill-desert,
and the consciousness that what
we have of good is due to
the grace of God.

CHARLES HODGE

So now there is no condemnation
for those who belong to Christ Jesus.

ROMANS 8:1 NLT

❧❧❧

The LORD is good to those who wait for Him,
to the soul who seeks Him.

LAMENTATIONS 3:25 NKJV

In the "No"

Father, please help me not to interpret
Your "no" answers to my prayers as Your not
working for my good. Remind me that You
are choosing to work in the way that is best.
I admit that I have trouble seeing the
"big picture" and sometimes my faith
wavers. In those times, help me to trust
that You are completing Your plan for me.
In Jesus' name, amen.

"You intended to harm me,
but God intended it for good to accomplish
what is now being done, the saving of many lives."

GENESIS 50:20 NIV

For it is God who works in you to will
and to act in order to fulfill his good purpose.

PHILIPPIANS 2:13 NIV

The LORD gives grace and glory;
no good thing does He withhold from
those who walk uprightly.

PSALM 84:11 NASB

The Christian does not think God will love us
because we are good, but that God will make us
good because He loves us; just as the roof of a sun
house does not attract the sun because it is bright,
but becomes bright because the sun shines on it.

C. S. LEWIS

❧

God never made a promise
that was too good to be true.

D. L. MOODY

❧

In biblical thinking, genuine love exists
only when good works are done in a context
where God rather than the doer gets the credit.

DANIEL FULLER

"Sovereign LORD, you are God!
Your covenant is trustworthy,
and you have promised these
good things to your servant."

2 SAMUEL 7:28 NIV

❧

We know that God's children do not make
a practice of sinning, for God's Son holds
them securely, and the evil one
cannot touch them.

1 JOHN 5:18 NLT

His Word My Hope Secures

> *Then He opened their minds to*
> *understand the scriptures.*
>
> LUKE 24:45 NASB

Instruction manuals come with most new
electronics and appliances. Some note the
best operating conditions. Others detail the
specifications of the unit and the parts. Still others
offer information on how to get assistance if the
device malfunctions or a repair or replacement
is needed. Unfortunately, most of us are guilty of
tossing the manual aside, saving it only for when
difficulty arises or troubleshooting is required.

God's Word should not be treated like an expendable instruction manual, consulted only when problems come or the occasional question arises. For the Bible is the instruction book that God gave us for life. His intention is that we read, study, and memorize it. The more we are familiar with what's inside it, the better we can know our God and His will for our lives.

God's Word is exciting. It is powerful. It offers comfort to His followers. It provides instruction for our Christian walk. Our loving Father has not left us on our own to figure things out. He has given us His Word to study, cherish, and follow daily.

I pray that God, the source of hope,
will fill you completely with joy and
peace because you trust in him.
Then you will overflow with confident hope
through the power of the Holy Spirit.

ROMANS 15:13 NLT

For in hope we have been saved,
but hope that is seen is not hope;
for who hopes for what he already sees?

ROMANS 8:24 NASB

Rejoice in our confident hope.
Be patient in trouble, and keep on praying.

ROMANS 12:12 NLT

The Bible is the inevitable outcome
of God's continuous speech. It is the
infallible declaration of His mind.

A. W. TOZER

❧

Do not study commentaries, lesson
helps or other books about the Bible:
study the Bible itself. Do not study
about the Bible, study the Bible.
The Bible is the Word of God,
and only the Bible is the
Word of God.

R. A. TORREY

❧

The Bible was not given to increase our
knowledge but to change our lives.

D. L. MOODY

As for me, I will always have hope;
I will praise you more and more.

PSALM 71:14 NIV

Why are you in despair, O my soul?
And why are you disturbed within me?
Hope in God, for I shall again praise Him,
the help of my countenance and my God.

PSALM 43:5 NASB

God's Enduring Word

Lord Jesus, thank You for Your Word.
It has endured throughout time, and
I know that it is just as relevant today
as it was centuries ago. Guide me to what
You want to teach me today. May I hide
Your words in my heart so that I not only
live a life more pleasing to You, but can pass
Your wisdom on to future generations.
May my life reflect Your truth. Amen.

Remember your promise to me;
it is my only hope.

PSALM 119:49 NLT

Therefore, with minds that are alert and fully sober,
set your hope on the grace to be brought to you
when Jesus Christ is revealed at his coming.

1 PETER 1:13 NIV

O Lord, you alone are my hope.
I've trusted you, O LORD, from childhood.

PSALM 71:5 NLT

The Word of God well understood and religiously
obeyed is the shortest route to spiritual perfection.
And we must not select a few favorite passages
to the exclusion of others. Nothing less than a
whole Bible can make a whole Christian.

A. W. TOZER

All the grace contained in [the Bible]
is owing to Jesus Christ as our Lord and Savior;
and, unless we consent to Him as our Lord we
cannot expect any benefit by Him as our Savior.

MATTHEW HENRY

But sanctify Christ as Lord in your hearts,
always being ready to make a defense
to everyone who asks you to give
an account for the hope that is in you,
yet with gentleness and reverence.

1 Peter 3:15 NASB

For in this hope we were saved.
But hope that is seen is no hope at all.
Who hopes for what they already have?
But if we hope for what we do not yet have,
we wait for it patiently.

Romans 8:24–25 NIV

In God's Word

Dear God, I ask that You renew my passion for
Your Word. Help me to open it daily and search
its treasures, to discover more of Your truths. May
it not be a task that I am in a hurry to accomplish.
I want to know You better through meditating on
Your wisdom. Help me to memorize portions of it.
Emblaze it upon my heart, as it is my guide
for life and enlightens my path. Amen.

Behold, the eye of the LORD is on those who fear Him,
on those who hope in His mercy.

PSALM 33:18 NKJV

I have been sent to proclaim faith
to those God has chosen and to teach them
to know the truth that shows them how to live
godly lives. This truth gives them confidence
that they have eternal life, which God—who does
not lie—promised them before the world began.

TITUS 1:1–2 NLT

May those who fear you rejoice when they see me,
for I have put my hope in your word.

PSALM 119:74 NIV

*He Will My Shield
and Portion Be*

My flesh and my heart may fail,
but God is the strength of my heart
and my portion forever.

PSALM 73:26 NIV

God is the shield and portion for His followers—
He is the defense and all-sufficient provision of
those who believe in Him.

The use of a shield implies that for Christians,
there will be times of attack. However, God hasn't
said, "I will give you a shield." He has declared,
"I will *be* your shield." He wants us to run to
Him, to hide behind Him as the battle intensifies.
Imagine children playing a game of tag. If there is
an adult nearby, the kid being chased might try to
hide behind the adult, creating a barrier between
himself and his chaser. That's what Christ wants to
be—the barrier between His beloved and the one
attempting to bring harm.

In Psalm 73:25, the psalmist asks, "Whom have I in heaven but you? And earth has nothing I desire besides you" (NIV). Thus God, our portion, is also our all-satisfying inheritance. He is the only thing that can truly make our souls sing with joy, now and forever!

When it feels as if you're in the line of fire, run to your Savior. He is a willing shield, ready to deflect any harm. And He is all we need. There is no end to Him, His love, or His goodness.

The LORD is good, a stronghold in the day of trouble;
and He knows those who trust in Him.

NAHUM 1:7 NKJV

"Who is like you, a people saved by the LORD?
He is your shield and helper and your glorious sword."

DEUTERONOMY 33:29 NIV

Spread out your petition before God,
and then say, "Thy will, not mine, be done."
The sweetest lesson I have learned
in God's school is to let the Lord choose for me.

D. L. MOODY

My life is a mystery which I do not attempt to really
understand, as though I were led by the hand in a
night where I see nothing, but can fully depend on
the love and protection of Him who guides me.

THOMAS MERTON

"My God is my rock, in whom I take refuge,
my shield and the horn of my salvation.
He is my stronghold, my refuge and my savior."

2 SAMUEL 22:3 NIV

But You, O LORD,
are a shield around me;
you are my glory,
the one who holds my head high.

PSALM 3:3 NLT

As for God, His way is perfect;
the word of the LORD is proven;
He is a shield to all who trust in Him.

PSALM 18:30 NKJV

God, My Shield

Heavenly Father, thank You for being my
shield of protection. I trust in You—I never
have to fear that anything will happen to
me that will catch You off guard. You protect
me from both seen and unseen dangers.
You are watchful on all sides and at all times.
Satan's fiery darts cannot penetrate Your
defenses. Thank You for being my safe place
where I can hide to escape the dangers
that threaten me. In Jesus' name, amen.

He will cover you with his feathers,
and under his wings you will find refuge;
his faithfulness will be your shield and rampart.

PSALM 91:4 NIV

⟨⟩

This inheritance is kept in heaven for you,
who through faith are shielded by God's power
until the coming of the salvation that is ready
to be revealed in the last time.

1 PETER 1:4–5 NIV

⟨⟩

And now I entrust you to God and the message
of his grace that is able to build you up and
give you an inheritance with all those
he has set apart for himself."

ACTS 20:32 NLT

The safest place in all
the world is in the will of God,
and the safest protection in all the
world is the name of God.

WARREN WIERSBE

Breathe in me, O Holy Spirit,
that my thoughts may all be holy.
Act in me, O Holy Spirit, that my work,
too, may be holy. Draw my heart,
O Holy Spirit, that I love but what
is holy. Strengthen me, O Holy Spirit,
to defend all that is holy. Guard me,
then, O Holy Spirit, that
I always may be holy.

SAINT AUGUSTINE OF HIPPO

But the God of Israel is no idol!
He is the Creator of everything that exists,
including Israel, his own special possession.
The LORD of Heaven's Armies is his name!

JEREMIAH 10:16 NLT

"The LORD is my portion," says my soul,
"Therefore I hope in Him!"

LAMENTATIONS 3:24 NKJV

God, My Portion

Dear Lord, Your Word tells me that You are
my portion, my inheritance. There is nothing
I need, in heaven or earth, other than You.
And, as my days pass, I find myself wanting
more and more of You. You are becoming
my only desire—for Your presence, Your
love, Your wisdom. Knowing that earth is
temporal and that You are all and in all, I have
great hope—in You! Thank You for being
the only portion I need—now and forever.
Amen.

He holds success in store for the upright,
he is a shield to those whose walk is blameless.

PROVERBS 2:7 NIV

You are my portion, LORD;
I have promised to obey your words.

PSALM 119:57 NIV

"O GOD the Lord, the strength of my salvation,
You have covered my head in the day of battle."

PSALM 140:7 NASB

A Life of Joy and Peace

May the God of hope fill you with all joy
and peace as you trust in him,
so that you may overflow with hope
by the power of the Holy Spirit.

ROMANS 15:13 NIV

What a pleasant thought! A life of *joy* and *peace*, words that typically appear in carols at Christmastime. Yet God desires that His children live lives characterized by joy and peace throughout the year.

The word *joy* is often equated with an outward sign of happiness. Although joy can be exhibited that way, it is more of a heart matter—one that may not necessarily be evidenced by a smile, but by a spirit of contentment, not to be based on happenings or circumstances but on the depth of our relationship with our Savior, the source of true joy.

Peace can be obtained and retained in moments of quiet solitude, and even in the midst of turmoil. For that peace is a state of restfulness, a quieting of the spirit. Christ Himself demonstrated the need to spend quiet time independently. He most often did so to talk with His Father. In the same way, we should imitate Christ's actions and set some quiet time aside to commune with Him. The more time we do, the more we will experience a life of joy and peace—before, during, and after the storm.

You will keep in perfect peace all who trust in you,
all whose thoughts are fixed on you!

ISAIAH 26:3 NLT

The mind governed by the flesh is death,
but the mind governed by the Spirit is life and peace.

ROMANS 8:6 NIV

Great peace have those who love your law,
and nothing can make them stumble.

PSALM 119:165 NIV

If you have no joy, there's a leak
in your Christianity somewhere.

BILLY SUNDAY

Our heart leaps for joy as we bow
before One who has never broken
His word or changed His purpose.

CHARLES SPURGEON

Joy is love exalted; peace is love in repose;
long-suffering is love enduring; gentleness is love
in society; goodness is love in action; faith is love
on the battlefield; meekness is love in school;
and temperance is love in training.

D. L. MOODY

If it is possible, as much as depends on you,
live peaceably with all men.

Romans 12:18 nkjv

"God blesses those who work for peace,
for they will be called the children of God."

Matthew 5:9 nlt

When a man's ways are pleasing to the Lord,
He makes even his enemies
to be at peace with him.

Proverbs 16:7 nasb

Always Joyful

Lord Jesus, it is my desire to be joyful in all things. Although not all situations will be pleasant, I can still choose to be joyful despite the emotions I'm feeling inside. Abiding in You, I can relax no matter where I am or what I do. In Your strength, I will make every effort to live a life of contentment, realizing that You are the source of my joy. In Your name, amen.

*Make every effort to live in peace
with everyone and to be holy;
without holiness no one will see the Lord.*

HEBREWS 12:14 NIV

*In peace I will both lie down and sleep, for You alone,
O LORD, make me to dwell in safety.*

PSALM 4:8 NASB

We are not at peace with others
because we are not at peace with
ourselves, and we are not at peace with
ourselves because we are not at peace
with God.

THOMAS MERTON

If you refuse to be hurried and pressed,
if you stay your soul on God, nothing
can keep you from that clearness of
spirit which is life and peace. In that
stillness you know what His will is.

AMY CARMICHAEL

*"For you will go out with joy
and be led forth with peace;
the mountains and hills
will break forth into shouts
of joy before you, and all
the trees of the field
will clap their hands."*

ISAIAH 55:12 NASB

❧

*Always be full of joy in the Lord.
I say it again—rejoice!*

PHILIPPIANS 4:4 NLT

❧

*No wonder my heart is glad, and I rejoice.
My body rests in safety.*

PSALM 16:9 NLT

The Peace of God

Father, on most days, peace seems elusive.
There are so many demands on my time
and energy, and if there is a quiet moment,
it is often spent preparing or planning
for another activity. I race from one
event to another, focused on what
needs to be accomplished next.
Please help me to find some time to
shut out all distractions and focus on You.
Bring peace to my body, mind, soul, and
spirit, I pray. In Jesus' name, amen.

Now may the Lord of peace himself give you
peace at all times and in every way.
The Lord be with all of you.

2 Thessalonians 3:16 niv

The Holy Spirit produces this kind of
fruit in our lives: love, joy, peace, patience,
kindness, goodness, faithfulness,
gentleness, and self-control.

Galatians 5:22 nlt

"You will live in joy and peace."

Isaiah 55:12 nlt

For the Kingdom of God is not a matter of what
we eat or drink, but of living a life of goodness
and peace and joy in the Holy Spirit.

Romans 14:17 nlt

But God...
Will Be Forever Mine

*There is a friend who sticks
closer than a brother.*

PROVERBS 18:24 NIV

God's Word tells us He always has been, is, and
always will be. He has no beginning, and He will
have no end. Our minds cannot comprehend that,
but it is comforting to rest in His steadfastness.

Yet as amazing as His *foreverness* is, His promises
go even further. He not only is a God who is not
bound by time, but He longs to have a relationship
for all eternity with the people He created. It now
becomes personal.

Just as God is pursuing His children, He wants us to pursue a relationship with Him. He eagerly desires our hearts to be fully His as we journey through life, seeking after Him. But the benefit of a relationship with Him doesn't end there. When the day comes for us to cross the line from the finite to the infinite, the connection continues. And we will then be present with the Savior in heaven forever!

God has promised you, His child, that when you call on Him, He will save you, and you will be forever His. Out of a heart of love for Him, you can happily declare that God is sticking with you from now until the end of time. He has been, is, and always will be "forever yours."

Now to the King eternal, immortal, invisible,
the only God, be honor and glory for ever and ever.
Amen.

1 TIMOTHY 1:17 NIV

For the wages of sin is death,
but the free gift of God
is eternal life through
Christ Jesus our Lord.

ROMANS 6:23 NLT

Before the mountains were brought forth,
or ever You had formed the earth and the world,
even from everlasting to everlasting,
You are God.

PSALM 90:2 NKJV

If any man is not sure that he is in
Christ, he ought not to be easy one
moment until he is sure. Dear friend,
without the fullest confidence as to
your saved condition, you have no
right to be at ease, and I pray you
may never be so. This is a matter too
important to be left undecided.

CHARLES SPURGEON

⁂

Jesus Christ became Incarnate
for one purpose, to make a way
back to God that man might stand
before Him as He was created to do,
the friend and lover of God Himself.

OSWALD CHAMBERS

And so it happened just as the Scriptures say:
"Abraham believed God, and God counted
him as righteous because of his faith."
He was even called the friend of God.

JAMES 2:23 NLT

"I am the LORD, and I do not change.
That is why you descendants of Jacob
are not already destroyed."

MALACHI 3:6 NLT

Friendship with God

Father God, we thank You that You are not
only our Savior, You are also our friend.
You, the perfect being, have sought to have
relationships with fallen, sinful man. You
have given all of Yourself, and it's Your desire
to have all of us. Thank You for choosing to
call me Your friend, even though I am less
than perfect. In Your name I pray, amen.

*For in Christ all the fullness of the
Deity lives in bodily form.*

COLOSSIANS 2:9 NIV

*And if the Spirit of him who raised
Jesus from the dead is living in you,
he who raised Christ from the dead
will also give life to your mortal bodies
because of his Spirit who lives in you.*

ROMANS 8:11 NIV

Treat the Lord Jesus Christ as a personal friend.
His is not a creed, a mere doctrine,
but it is He Himself we have.

D. L. MOODY

If Christ has died for me—ungodly as I am,
without strength as I am—then I can
no longer live in sin, but must arouse
myself to love and serve Him
who has redeemed me.
I cannot trifle with the evil that
killed my best Friend.
I must be holy for his sake.
How can I live in sin when
He has died to save me from it?

CHARLES SPURGEON

Now hope does not disappoint,
because the love of God
has been poured out in our
hearts by the Holy Spirit
who was given to us.

ROMANS 5:5 NKJV

"Greater love has no one than this:
to lay down one's life for one's friends."

JOHN 15:13 NIV

Included in Eternity

Lord God, I cannot begin to understand how
You could have no beginning and no end. For
everything I see on this earth has a start and
a finish. But I thank You that You loved me
enough to include me in Your eternity.
I eagerly await the time that I will pass
over from this earth to Your glorious heaven.
My praise to You, although begun here,
will continue forever. Amen.

Jesus Christ is the same yesterday
and today and forever.

<small>HEBREWS 13:8 NASB</small>

Come close to God, and
God will come close to you.
Wash your hands, you sinners;
purify your hearts, for your loyalty
is divided between God and the world.

<small>JAMES 4:8 NLT</small>

When We've Been There
Ten Thousand Years

A day is like a thousand years to the Lord,
and a thousand years is like a day.

2 PETER 3:8 NLT

Ten thousand years! Considering that from a human
perspective, it seems like a long time. But God's
system is a different one—so contrary to what
we experience. He does not have to glance at a
wristwatch or take a peek at a cell phone to stay on
schedule. The seconds and minutes do not get away
from Him.

How liberating it would be to go on a vacation
and not be constrained by time. To remove your
watch and simply enjoy the day certainly promotes
relaxation. Most of us would want to stay and
enjoy the freedom of this kind of lifestyle as long
as possible. But eventually there is a return to
schedules and deadlines. Once again, we're forced
to consult our dials and digital displays.

In heaven, there will never be any more darkness. No more clocks. All of the days dictated by a timepiece will be a thing of the past. Time will cease to exist. We will simply be with our Savior. We will reunite with loved ones and meet other believers. There will be singing—true worship. There will be feasting. And there will be joy. . .joy like we have never known before.

"You, Lord, in the beginning laid the foundation of the earth, and the heavens are the works of Your hands; they will perish, but You remain; and they all will become old like a garment, and like a mantle You will roll them up; like a garment they will also be changed. But You are the same, and Your years will not come to an end."

HEBREWS 1:10–12 NASB

Eternity to the godly is a day that has
no sunset; eternity to the wicked is
a night that has no sunrise.

THOMAS WATSON

The best moment of a Christian's life is
his last one, because it is the one that is
nearest heaven. And then it is that he
begins to strike the keynote of the song
which he shall sing to all eternity.

CHARLES SPURGEON

Jesus said to her, "I am the resurrection
and the life. He who believes in Me, though he
may die, he shall live. And whoever lives and
believes in Me shall never die."

John 11:25–26 NKJV

After that, we who are still alive and
are left will be caught up together
with them in the clouds to meet
the Lord in the air. And so we
will be with the Lord forever.

1 Thessalonians 4:17 NIV

No More Time

Father, my mind is limited by earthly time,
so it is difficult for me to even begin to
imagine eternity. My waking is ruled by the
clock, as are events and meals throughout
the day. And time dictates what time I go
to bed. But in heaven, there will be no need
for sleeping or eating. There will be no
obligations. There will be no darkness.
I long for the joy of spending eternity
with You! In Jesus' name, amen.

"Don't let your hearts be troubled.
Trust in God, and trust also in me.
There is more than enough room in my Father's home.
If this were not so, would I have told you
that I am going to prepare a place for you?
When everything is ready, I will come and get you,
so that you will always be with me where I am."

JOHN 14:1–3 NLT

And this is the promise that He has
promised us—eternal life.

1 JOHN 2:25 NKJV

Rejoice, that the immortal God is born,
so that mortal man may
live in eternity.

JOHN HUSS

I judge all things only by the price
they shall gain in eternity.

JOHN WESLEY

Christ is the desire of nations,
the joy of angels,
the delight of the Father.
What solace then must that
soul be filled with, that has the
possession of Him to all eternity!

JOHN BUNYAN

Now Christ has gone to heaven.
He is seated in the place of honor next to God,
and all the angels and authorities
and powers accept his authority.

1 PETER 3:21–22 NLT

One thing I have asked from the LORD,
that I shall seek: that I may dwell
in the house of the LORD
all the days of my life,
to behold the beauty of the LORD
and to meditate in His temple.

PSALM 27:4 NASB

My New Home

Father, thank You for Your graciousness in preparing a place for me in Your presence. My days on earth have been blessed. You have given me family and friends to love. I have enjoyed Your creation. But the best is yet to come! You have promised to take me to a place where all of Your children will be together, where we will experience a new earth and be with You forever. In Jesus' name, amen.

*Listen, I tell you a mystery: We will not all sleep,
but we will all be changed—in a flash, in the twinkling
of an eye, at the last trumpet. For the trumpet will
sound, the dead will be raised imperishable, and we will
be changed. For the perishable must clothe itself with
the imperishable, and the mortal with immortality.
When the perishable has been clothed with the
imperishable, and the mortal with immortality,
then the saying that is written will come true:
"Death has been swallowed up in victory."*

1 CORINTHIANS 15:51–54 NIV

We've No Less Days...
Than When We'd First Begun

Praise the LORD. Praise God in his sanctuary;
praise him in his mighty heavens.

PSALM 150:1 NIV

God created us to worship Him and have a
relationship with Him. He longs to hear our words
and songs of praise. He alone deserves our endless
adoration. He is the glorious God who will never
leave us, the gracious Savior who has prepared a
special place for us, and the Holy Spirit who will
forever guide us.

When a believer leaves this world and enters
heaven, he will begin his song of praise to our
three-in-one God. The new song will begin and
have no end. This act of adoration will not be a
task-oriented performance; it will flow from a heart
full of love for God.

Here on earth, the believer's communication with the Lord is through prayer—the conduit through which we worship Him, make requests of Him, confess our faults to Him, and thank Him. But on entry into heaven, there will be a new way to communicate. We will be in His presence and able to speak directly to Him! There will be no more requests or confessions—simply worship and thanksgiving.

Our desire to worship the God who showered us with grace will be a natural one. We will put our love for Him into word and song—true praise of the One who saved us and loves us with an everlasting love.

To the only God our Savior be glory,
majesty, power and authority,
through Jesus Christ our Lord,
before all ages, now and forevermore! Amen.

JUDE 1:25 NIV

Let them praise Your great and
awesome name—He is holy.

PSALM 99:3 NKJV

With my mouth I will give thanks
abundantly to the LORD; and
in the midst of many I will praise Him.

PSALM 109:30 NASB

A Joyful Noise

Lord God, how exciting to imagine the praise
and worship that we will be a part of in
heaven. The angels will be there in addition
to every person who has called upon
You as Lord and Savior. All voices together
will be singing and shouting praises to You.
How I look forward to being a part of that
heavenly choir, adding my contribution of
a "joyful noise." In Jesus' name, amen.

Praise the LORD, my soul;
all my inmost being, praise his holy name.
Praise the LORD, my soul, and forget not all his benefits—
who forgives all your sins and heals all your diseases,
who redeems your life from the pit and crowns you
with love and compassion, who satisfies your desires with
good things so that your youth is renewed like the eagle's.

PSALM 103:1–5 NIV

Praise is the rehearsal of our eternal song.
By grace we learn to sing, and in glory we continue
to sing. What will some of you do when you get to
heaven, if you go on grumbling all the way?
Do not hope to get to heaven in that style.
But now begin to bless the name of the Lord.

<small>CHARLES SPURGEON</small>

If you had a thousand crowns you should
put them all on the head of Christ!
And if you had a thousand tongues
they should all sing his praise,
for he is worthy!

<small>WILLIAM TIPTAFT</small>

Exalt the Lord our God!
Bow low before his feet, for he is holy!

PSALM 99:5 NLT

"You alone are the Lord.
You have made the heavens,
the heaven of heavens with all their host,
the earth and all that is on it,
the seas and all that is in them.
You give life to all of them
and the heavenly host
bows down before You."

NEHEMIAH 9:6 NASB

Let my mouth be filled with Your praise
and with Your glory all the day.

PSALM 71:8 NKJV

Eternal Worship

Heavenly Father, I do not want to wait until I get to heaven to bless You with the honor that is due You. I will begin my song and worship now, showing my appreciation for Your love and grace while I am here. Many people throughout history have used music to honor You, and I gladly join them. Then, when You call me home, I will be an eager choir member, singing to You for all eternity. Amen.

"We give thanks to you,
Lord God Almighty,
the One who is and who was,
because you have taken
your great power and
have begun to reign."

REVELATION 11:17 NIV